Written, illustrated, edited,
designed, typeset, published,
marketed and distributed
by

the Children of
St. Augustine's
Primary School,
Coatbridge.

~

*Tolle Lege is a Latin phrase commonly associated
with St. Augustine and chosen many years ago as the
school motto. Originally referring to the Bible, it
means **pick up and read.***

First published in 2004 by
Jam Neck,
c/o St. Augustine's Primary School,
Henderson Street,
Coatbridge ML5 1BL

in association with
Jam Jar Lurker & Son,
www.jamjarlurker.com

ISBN 0-9538806-2-1

Printed and bound by CPI Bath.

Contents

Front Cover *~ Adam Flynn*
Gallery 1 *~ Caitlin Young, Helen Webster, Colette Sullivan, Brian Boyle, Emma Donald, Lynsay Wallace, Christopher Honeyman & Emma McAleer*
Gallery 2 *~ Keir McGill, Lisa McDade, Iain Kane, Katie McLaughlin, Rachael Maxwell, Martin Chisholm, Garrett Leckie & Barry McLees*
Back Cover *~ text by Peter Donaldson; illustration by David White*

Preface
by Jane McAleer,
headteacher of St. Augustine's.

This anthology of stories and poems is a great testimony to the literary skills of the children of St. Augustine's Primary School - from the very youngest to the oldest in the school.

As parents and educators we cannot help to be impressed, in this volume, by the insightful phrases, comments and in-depth knowledge and thoughts of our young people - the "literary masters" of tomorrow!

A truly fine publication this book also highlights the artistic talents of our pupils and serves to promote the idea that literature and art together can produce excellence.

Based on an inspirational idea by Mr O'Dowd this work has afforded our children an opportunity to trace the path of a piece of literature from its conception to its publication - experiencing along the way the highs and lows of the publishing world!

A literary first for St. Augustine's but hopefully not the last, this anthology may be the springboard for other excellent achievements - could another J. K. Rowling be uncovered in St. Augustine's we must ask ourselves? Whatever future masterpieces are produced by our children one thing is certain - the talents of our children must always be encouraged and developed to ensure that they fulfil their potential. This wonderful collection of stories and poems recognises this fundamental aim.

I commend this publication to you and wish you many happy hours browsing through its delightful contents with your family and friends.

J. Mc Aleer

Foreword
by Des Dillon,
award-winning novelist, poet and playwright (and the brother of our very own Mrs McLean).

Dear Kids,

It was great reading your stories and poems. I read some out to Bailey the Lurcher and Connor the Collie. They said to say woof. Finnigan, Molly and Steve the cats all say purr.

I'm not going to single out anybody for praise although there were one or two which impressed me very much. What I did get was an insight into your fears and concerns both local and global. I shared in your hopes through your daydreams and wishes. Thought your thoughts both surreal and sometimes all too real. Visited incidents in your lives good and bad. But most of all I admired your IMAGINATION. Imagination is the key to good storytelling. It helps us to exaggerate and create vivid images for the reader. Writing without using your imagination is like going downhill on a skateboard with no wheels.

So keep on using that imagination - keep on telling the stories. It is important that children get to tell their own stories. That they learn their lives are magic too. And how important stories are in life. Here's a wee test - see how long it is from this point until somebody tells you a story. I think you'll be surprised by the amount of stories we tell each other in a day. Whether it's what happened at the shops, on the news or some mad story we just made up for the sake of it, stories are how we communicate. And never more so than in the Irish-Scot community of Coatbridge - where two great storytelling cultures come together.

All best wishes.

Galloway
Sunday, 21 March 2004

Introduction
by the Editorial Team

Joseph   **N**icole
Anton   **E**mma
Mark   **C**hristopher
    Colette
    Kerri

Welcome to our book of stories,
Inside you'll find a lot of glories.
Stories and poems from all ages,
Children's work fills these pages.
Happy, scary, exciting, sad,
Stories that will drive you mad,
Creatures that you've never seen,
Blue, orange and even green.
Look inside and you will find
Stories that will blow your mind.
A lot of work went into this book,
Now we hope you'll take a look.

~

We would like to thank
Des Dillon, Charlie Tait,
the staff of St. Augustine's,
everyone who pre-ordered the book
and all the companies who generously sponsored us.

Emma McAleer   Nicole Mulholland   Colette Sullivan
Joseph Weatherall   Anton Traquair   Kerri McKay   Christopher Muller
Mark Hughes

Primary 1

Katie McLaughlin

I like to go out and
play in my garden

Rebecca Cowell

I like being on
a ship going
to Ireland

Gabriel Leonard

I like Play with my
friends in my garden

Monica Toal

I like when it is christmas Eve.

Rebecca McNamee

I like to cuddle my guinea pigs.

Aoife Bradley

I like going to the park.

Emma Constable

I like to go out for
dinner with my mum dad. and
little sister

Chloe McCabe

I Like to play weth my power rangers.

Jonathan Watt

I like to play out in my garden.

Ruth Trower

I Like going to parties with my MUM

Marcella Foy

I feel happy.
I am going to colettes party.

Emma Henderson

I felt sad when
I lost my favourite toy.
It was a Piglet.

Eve Elder

I feel sad because someone put my drawing in the bin.

Piero Marcuccilli

I am feeling happy because my mum and dad are taking me to the carnival.

Tieghan McMullan

I feel sad. My dad is going to Brazil.

Lucy Armour

I feel happy when my sister plays with me.

Jonathan Hughes

I feel sad when my dad goes away without me.

Adam Watt

My loose Tooth
by Harry Sharpe

Last year when my little sister was in bed and I was down with my mum and dad I felt that my tooth had fallen out. When I put it under my pillow the tooth fairy came. She took the tooth away and put a pound coin under my pillow. I slept happy all night. When I woke up I saw the pound coin. I was very happy.

My Wobbly Tooth
by Emily Drummond

Last year in my house I had a wobbly tooth. I bumped into the door and tripped over my toy. I was sad. Then the tooth fairy came and I was happy.

Watching the Fireworks
by Ben Plant

Last year on a Monday, at the park, me and my mum were watching fireworks. I was very excited. Then I went to my dad, 'Dad! Dad!' I saw lots of fireworks and they were very colourful.'

Emma Donald

Harry's Seal
by Danielle McFadyen

One day Harry was going to the pet shop. When they got there, Harry's mum said, 'What about a snake?'

'But I want a seal,' said Harry.

'Ok,' said Harry's mum.

When they got home Harry said, 'Where is the seal going to sleep?'

Harry's mum said, 'In the pond.'

Harry's Elephant
by Christopher Arcari

Harry's mum said, 'What do you want?'

'I want an Elephant.'

Harry's mum said, 'You can't get an elephant.'

Harry said, 'But Mum, that is the only thing I want.'

Harry went home and fell asleep and Harry's mum slammed the door and woke him up.

Lucy Hughes

My Boxing Tooth
by Antonia Donaldson

Yesterday me and my dad and gran were going shopping. When we came back I asked if I was allowed to go out. My gran said yes. I went out but I didn't notice my dad playing boxing and he knocked me over. My tooth fell out. It was very exciting.

Lost on the Beach
by Damian Hamilton

A long time ago when I was on holiday I went to the beach with my dad. I wanted to make a sandcastle. Someone shouted on me and I looked behind me. I turned to my dad's side but he was gone. I did a silly thing and went looking for him. Then my dad found me. I was happy to see him.

The Chocolate Tooth
by Dominic Boon

On Saturday I was watching Dick and Dom, and I took a bit of Dairy Milk and my tooth was sore and my tooth fell out. That night I put my tooth under the pillow. When I woke up the next morning I had five pounds under my pillow. I was very happy.

Keir McGill

Victoria's Tooth
by Samantha Cairns

On Friday a little girl in Primary One called Victoria was going to school. It was lunch time and she had finished her sandwiches. So she ate her apple. Her tooth became slack. Then the bell rang for hometime. She ran to her mum and said, 'My tooth is slack.'

Her mum said, 'If it falls out, put it under your pillow.'

So that night she went to bed and her tooth came out. She said, 'I shall do what my mum said.' So she put her tooth under her pillow and went to sleep. That night the tooth fairy came. In the morning she woke up and looked under her pillow and there was a twenty pound note. She was happy and went to show her baby sister, her mum and dad. Her mum and dad said, 'Well done.'

She was very, very happy.

The Haircut
by Michael Robertson

A boy called Joe did not want to get his hair cut. He went. It was fun. He was happy. Joe got a lollypop for sitting good.

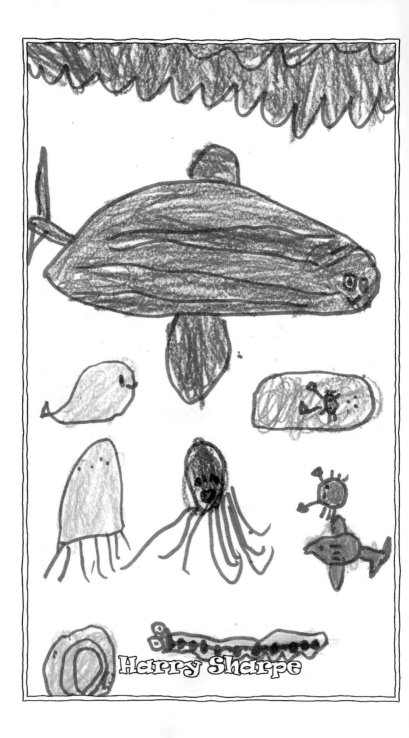

Lost in Asda
by Robbie Lyons

One day a boy called Jack went to Asda. Jack was scared because he was lost. It was getting near dark and Jack saw a shadow in the distance. He got closer and closer and Jack saw his mum and dad. Jack got a row but he was happy.

Finding Sea Shells
by Niamh Bree

In the Summer a big girl called Lorraine went to the beach to find loads and loads of seashells. She went because it was a very sunny day. When it was time to go home she made a picture for her gran. Her gran loved the picture.

Nesta and Ned
by Victoria Renwick

One day Nesta and Ned went to Wild Wood because they were bored. So they went and had fun. But then it became dark and they got lost. They saw a bird. The bird said to Nesta and Ned, 'Are you lost?'

'Yes' said Nesta and Ned. 'We are lost.' So the bird took Nesta and Ned home.

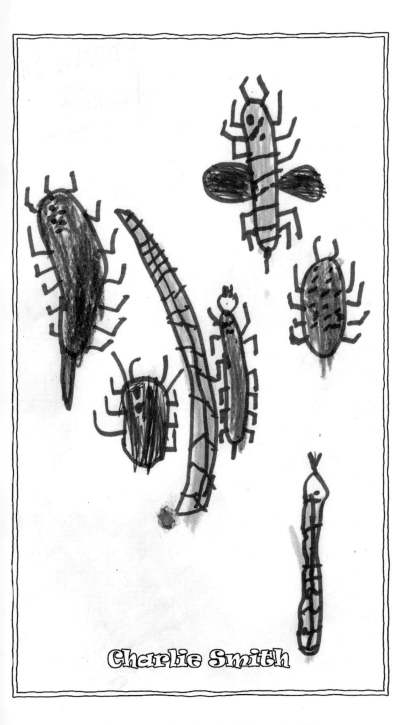

Charlie Smith

Lost in Music
by Erin Kellet

One day a girl called Janine went to Asda with her mum. Her dad was waiting in the car. She asked her mum if she could go and see the videos. Her mum said 'Yes.' So off Janine went. Dad thought they were taking too long. Mum went to get milk. Janine moved to see the CDs. She then realised her mum was not there. She was sad and scared. Then her mum went to the CDs. She saw her and they were happy.

Tutankhamun
by Jodi Livingston
and Nicole Millar

Tutankhamun was an Egyptian king.
He had slaves that did everything.
As a child he would laugh and sing.
At nine years old he took the throne,
He was a pharaoh from that day on.
Sadly he died, got wrapped up and tied.
I wish he were alive.

Best Friends
by Colette McKeown

At nursery my best friends were Leah, Nicole and
Lisa, but my best best friend was Katie. We always
had fun together and we never fell out. One day we
went to the toilet and we flooded the sink. We had
so much fun together. One day we went out to play
with our kite. Katie had short black hair, and had
green eyes. We made paper butterflies. She will be
my best friend for ever and ever.

Mark McKeown

The Sad Snowman
by Emma Burke

On a cold winter's day I woke up and looked out of the window. I was excited. Outside was a white sparkling blanket of snow. I woke my mum and we went and made a snowman. I was delighted with my snowman, but it was my bedtime so I kissed it goodnight. The next day I went out to see my snowman, but it had melted. I was sad and on the ground where the snowman had been there was a puddle and some stones.

It said, 'I love you Emma.'

Friends Forever
Lisa McDade

In Spain about a year ago,
I was at the pool playing with my ball,
When I saw a nice girl.
She had black hair and brown eyes.
I looked at her and she looked at me,
Brown eyes staring at blue eyes,
Blue eyes staring at brown.
I went to ask her if she wanted to be my friend,
And she said yes.
And now she is my pen pal.
I told her my name,
And she said her name was Laura.
We will be friends forever.

The Best Winter Ever
by Fiona Robertson

One cold winter's day as I woke, I looked out the
window. It was snowing. I was so excited. I ran
outside. I went to see if my best friend was coming
out. We went round my back. We built a snowman.
We called him Snowy. That night my friend and I had
a sleepover. It was time to go to bed. When my friend
and I were sleeping, we heard a noise coming from
outside. We put our dressing gowns on and our
slippers and we ran outside. Snowy began to talk to us
and he asked us if we wanted to go a ride with him.
We said, 'Yes!' We went for a ride through the town
and then he took us home. The next day as we woke
up we went outside and the sun was out. We saw a
puddle and in the puddle there was a message from
Snowy. It said , 'I will always love you.' My friend
and I were very sad.

One Day I Went Out and Played
by Rachael Weatherall

One day I went out and played.
There was a thing and it swung.
And then I saw that it could swing with someone on it
And I went and played on it
And it was great fun,
So it was.

Darryl Boyle

Roundabout
by Evan McGill

One day when I went out to play
I saw something new.
It was round and it went round,
And its name was the same.
One day when I went out to play I saw a roundabout.
It sat where I used to play and sat there for a day.

The Land of
Light Fluffy Fun
by Lisa McDade

Slices of white magic flew past my window pane,
I looked out of my window
And I heard someone call my name,
I ran down to the garden to see just who was there,
I saw a snowman at the gate
And I couldn't believe he was there,
But he melted at the gate,
I was sad to be there.

Snowflakes
by Jodi Livingston & Emma Burke

Snowflakes, snowflakes whirling round,
Wait till they touch it;
Wait till they touch the ground.
Snowflakes, snowflakes whirling round and round,
Snowflakes sparkling on the ground.

Rachael Weatherall

The Snow
by Niall Quinn Thomas

Snow, snow,
People make snowmen,
Snow, snow,
People make snowballs,
Snow, snow,
We play in it,
Snow, snow,
We make snow angels,
Snow, snow,
We make footprints,
Snow, snow,
We throw it,
Snow, we love it.

My Best Friend
by Emma Armour

My best friend is called Roisin. I met her in Primary One. Me and Roisin have the same talents, like ice-skating which we do every Thursday night. Sometimes we make nicknames for each other. I am Emzer and Roisin is Posh. Roisin has brownie blondish hair and blue eyes. Roisin is quite small. Roisin is a tiny bit older than me but we are still friends. Roisin is very funny and that's what I like about her. If I was not moving house I would be happy because Roisin is moving up near the house I am moving out of! Roisin and me are even going to work with each other; we are going to be opticians. If Roisin had to move to Italy, I would cry until I was dead!

Leah Watson

Shannon Kinsella

The Swimming Necklace
by Roisin Hughes

Last year I was with my dad my sister and my brothers. We were at the swimming baths. My sister and me shared a locker and my dad and my brothers shared a locker. Once I got into the pool I swam and swam and swam.

My dad said, 'You're splashing water in my eyes.'

So I stopped splashing his eyes with water, and suddenly my necklace snapped. I was so sad.

My dad said, 'Give it to me and I'll try and fix it.' But he couldn't fix it this time. I was very, very, very sad.

When I was getting changed to go home my dad said, 'Don't worry I'll glue it together.' I still had a great time even though my necklace snapped. It was a great day!

Going Swimming
by Joseph Cassidy

On the October week holiday I went with my gran and my sister Anna to the Time Capsule. First I went to the waterfall and I swam right through it. Then I went just beside the river rapids.

The water was so strong it felt like I was being blown away. Then I went to the spaceship, the rain was pouring down. We went back down as the storm was starting and there were huge waves going up and down and up and down.

I loved it all. I had such a good time I went back the next day.

I Wish
by James McDonald

I wish I was invisible
So my brother couldn't hit me,
I wish I could play for Scotland
And win the World Cup,
I wish gran would come back to Earth
So I could see her,
I wish I were a millionaire
So I could own a giant factory,
I wish I could turn into anything,
Then I could fly,
I wish I was super fast
So I could be in the Olympics.

Time in the Capsule
Reece Doherty

Last night my sister, my dad and me went to the Time Capsule. First we went in the rocket and then we went on the flumes. But when we went on the flumes, because we came at night the flumes were all dark. It was dark and when we came to the dip it lit up again.

When we came out my dad asked, 'Do you want a bag of crisps?' My sister and me said yes. So my dad put some money in, one packet of crisps fell out and straight after another fell out without putting any money in.

I said, 'How did that happen?'

Then my dad said, 'We must be lucky.'

I had fun, the swimming was good.

My Best Friend
by Chloe Street

My best friend is called Mairead. I met her in Primary One. She has green eyes and curly red hair and she is big and she is most of all pretty. She is very funny and we like to play schools. She is very kind too. I am very lucky to have a friend like her.

If she had to move away from me I would be very sad.

Imagine
by Louisa Irvine

Imagine your head got stuck in the shed,
Imagine a clown wearing a crown,
Imagine the sun looked like a bun,
Imagine a bear lost all his hair.

Danielle McCaul

Jodie Livingstone

Imagine
by Rachel Agnew

Imagine a giraffe having a bath,
Imagine a spoon flew to the moon,
Imagine a squirrel turned into a girl,
Imagine a fish making a wish,
Imagine a pig doing a jig.

Imagine
by Lee Cunningham

Imagine a cow getting a row,
Imagine a pig wearing a wig,
Imagine a goat sailing a boat,
Imagine a bee looking at me.

Paddy the Dog
by Jennifer Traynor

Paddy
the
dog
jumped
over
the
log
and
landed
in
the
fog
and
came
back
home
and
said
to me,
'What
is
for
tea
because
I
am
hungree.'

A Letter to Santa
by Rachel Craig

Santa Claus,
The North Pole,
Iceland.

Dear Santa,

For Christmas I would really like a computer, Playstation 2, skates and felt tip pens. And I want to make a promise, I will be good, and help my whole family and say my prayers.

Thank you.
Your special friend,

Rachel

Furry Insect
By Luke Mullen

Insect, insect you are furry,
Always flying in a hurry,
Flying in my room,
Going zoom, zoom, zoom.

You think you're scary,
But you're only hairy,
Eating leaves you collect,
You're my little insect.

Cold Feet
by Melissa Crofton

Last December I went to the Lochs with my mum. I put my woolly hat on my head and my favourite gloves with gold spots.

My mum said, 'Are you nice and warm?'

I said, 'My toes are a bit cold but I am alright'.

We were walking along the edge and we saw some children on the ice with a big sledge. I saw a notice and it said **DANGEROUS, NO ICE SKATING**. Then my brother and my dad turned up and my brother brought his ball with him, and kicked it onto the ice.

He said, 'Dad, go and get it please.'

So my dad went to get it and he fell in. Then we phoned the emergency services and they got my dad out and we were all happy.

Flowers and Chocolates
by Kenedi McMullen

It all began last night, when I was out playing with my sister building a snowman. There are a lot of houses about in my street and it is very peaceful. A lot of old people live there. An old lady was walking by with a heavy bag of shopping and there were boys walking about.

They ran into the old lady and she fell, everything fell out of her bag and she was badly hurt. My sister and I did not know what to do. I had my mobile with me, so I phoned an ambulance and the police came too.

The old lady, Mrs. Rose, went into the hospital. My sister and I got her some flowers and chocolates. We asked her how she was feeling and she was fine. She got out of hospital the next day and came to stay at my house till she got better and she did.

Insect Fright
by Lynzi Robertson

Insect, insect big and tall,
I like the way you like to crawl,
Up the wall you go at night,
Always giving me a fright.

Crash!
by Jennifer Traynor

Last winter, I was sitting in my bedroom and I saw orange lights reflecting on the wall. I went to my window and it was a gritter. I thought to myself it must be slippy. I started to read my book when I heard a **Crash!** I got the fright of my life.

I ran to my window. There was a car upside down and the gritter was trapped between a wall and the car. I ran to my mum and dad and said, 'There has been an accident.'

My mum said, 'What will we do?'

I said, 'Get help.' I phoned the emergency services and they got the man who was trapped out of the car.

I was happy that no one was hurt. I got a medal for being calm and I was very very happy. The man who was in the car gave me £100.

Insects With Wings
by Dylan Fenwick

Insects, insects big and small,
Some very thin and some very tall,
Some with wings and some with none at all,
As I was saying, with wings and with none at all,
But my favourite insects would have to be
Ones that crawl.

Aaahhhhhh!!!!
by Declan McVeigh

It all happened last Tuesday. That was the day that I had my accident. That day we all got ready for gym. We walked into the hall, then we ran about the hall and then Miss Campbell said, 'One, two, three, jump.' I jumped up in the sky like a rocket and I came down with a big **CRASH!**

I shouted, *'AAHHHHHH!!!!'* I was in agony.

Miss Campbell came running as fast as she could. She took me to the office and I thought I had broken my arm. My mum came to my school. She took me to the hospital and I had to get a plaster cast and a sling and when I got to school they all wrote on the plaster cast and we had fun.

The Magic Lake
by Mark Docherty

Last October, me, my two sisters and my mum and my dad all went to see my aunt and uncle. When we got there, my uncle asked us if we wanted to see the magic lake. When we got there it was the most fantastic thing we had ever seen.

It had evergreen trees and some trees had colours of russet, copper, gold and yellow. The lake was very calm and it stretched for miles. There were rabbits and squirrels running through the bushes.

I asked my uncle why the lake was magical. He said at night magic unicorns and magic fish came out of the water. I went to the lake at night and I saw magical unicorns and fish. Then I went back inside because I was frightened.

My Accident at School
by Anton Lafferty

Last Tuesday at school, our class were going to gym and Miss Campbell said, 'Let's get ready for our warm up.' Miss Campbell was shouting

'One, two, three, jump.' This is when my accident happened.

I jumped high and then **THUD, CRASH!** I thought I had dislocated my arm. I was yelling and I had fallen onto the chairs. Miss Campbell just slammed down her beater.

Miss Campbell took me to the office and my mum came and took me to the hospital. The doctor gave me a big plaster. When I got back to school the children signed my plaster and I felt better.

Bertie the Bug
by Amy McKenna

Bertie the bug climbs on my wall,
Not fat, not thin, but very tall,
He always smiles and crawls on the street,
Loves to eat, but he's got smelly feet,
Big blue eyes with white disguise,
If you see him, he will give you a surprise,
Flies in the sun but not in the rain,
Or sunbathes on my windowpane,
Sprawls and crawls all over the floor,
When he sleeps he snores on my door.

Falling Through the Ice
Catherine Locke

Last December, my dad and I were at the Lochs. It was a really cold day but we were nice and warm. My dad said, 'Make sure you put your hat, scarf and gloves on.'

I was wearing my favourite hat which had a little horse on it. My scarf had one too because they came in a set. My gloves had little black spots on them.

My dad and I were talking to each other about how cold the ducks would be. Then we noticed two little boys on the ice, and they had a sledge. My dad tapped me and said that he could see a notice that said **NO ICE SKATING!** I heard something. I told my dad because it sounded like someone shouting HELP! My dad got out his mobile and called the emergency services. They got the children out and my dad and I got a medal for saving the children. It was very good because my dad got me some sweets from the shop.

The Street Accident
by Paul Gibson

It all began last winter when I was in my room and snow started falling from the sky. I had just finished playing my computer game called 101 Dalmations and just then the computer went off and I said to myself there must be a power cut. I told my sister who was sitting next to me and just then I saw orange flashing lights and then heard a big crash.

I looked out of my window, then I looked closer and I saw a car between a wall and a very big truck. So I ran downstairs and told my parents. They phoned the emergency services.

They came and got the two people out of the car and the head of the emergency services said that it was a very brave thing to do and he gave me a medal.

I said, 'Thank you.'

And he said, 'You're welcome'

Sweets
by Ryan Diamond

Sour, sweet and soft,
We love them,
Enormous sometimes,
Egg shaped,
Tangy, tasty,
Sometimes sick!

The Little Insect
by Amber Sneddon

Insect, insect, climbing up a wall,
Please be careful you don't fall,
If you do, you'll hurt your head,
And you will have to go to bed.

My Cat With the Hat
by Amy Louise Robertson

My cat
  with the hat
    likes a
      good old pat.
My cat
  with the hat
    can do
      lots of
        good tricks
          and he'll
            show you
              just that.

At the
  end of
    the day
      he stops
        the good
          play and
          with a
            tip of
              his hat
          he gives
        me a pat.

The Mischievous Cat Jess
by Katie Boyle

Once there was a mischievous cat who always got into trouble. He lived in a small cottage with his owner Catherine, who called him Jess. The first day he lived with Catherine he was very hungry from travelling to the little cottage. He was given a saucer of milk and instead of drinking it, like any normal cat, he stood in it and it spilled all over the kitchen floor. Jess then ran through the milk and ran around the house making a mess.

The milk was quite slippy, so when Jess tried to stop he couldn't. He slid into the washing machine. Luckily, Catherine just came into room. She had just started the washing machine when she noticed a little black tail. Catherine stopped the washing machine as quickly as she could and out Jess jumped. 'Oh Jess!' said Catherine.

The Insect's Mummy
by Sian McMullan

Insect, insect why do you hurry?
Through the bushes you always scurry,
Insect, insect don't you worry!
You're safe beside your mummy.

Insect, Insect
Rachel Irving

Insect, insect why do you fly?
You fly so beautifully in the sky.
My, my, what a fly can view!
From up high in the sky so blue.

Insect, insect what do you see?
As you go buzzing past me,
My, my, how a fly can go!
Swiftly dashing to and fro.

Insect, insect when will you land?
And settle for a moment on my hand.
My, my, if you wait a little a longer,
You might feel so much stronger.

1st Place
by Amy McKenna

Last year on the 1st of March 2003, I was in a
dancing competition with all of my dancing class.
I went to Airdrie Town Hall with my family and
one of my friends. That was where my dancing
competition was. First the wee babies went on to
the stage and did their solo. After that, my group
went on the stage and performed our solo. It was
the same for every other group. When the other
people were finished doing their solo, my dancing
teacher Michelle announced the awards. She told
the babies first and then she announced my
group's awards. I was very excited. My dancing

teacher told us 3rd place, 2nd place and then she said, '1st place, Amy McKenna!'

My mum was crying with joy. My dad said to my mum, 'Amy's won a prize. It's brilliant, but you don't have to cry.' It was a gold trophy.

Just then my dancing teacher Michelle shouted, 'Come and do your duet.' We all did our duet. Then Michelle said, 'All come over here.' We all went over and she called out the best people in the dancing class. She called out some people and shouted, 'Amy McKenna!' My mum was crying again with joy. When Michelle had called out all the best people we had a disco. After the disco was over we all went home. I took my trophies home. My friend's mum and dad came over to congratulate me for winning so many trophies. They were delighted. That night I sat my trophies in my room and I have still got them there. I'll never forget that day.

The Hairy Insect
Shannon Kerrigan

Insect, insect in a hurry,
Flying through trees,
Flying through bushes,
Why do you always hurry?
Flying in my room,
Zoom, zoom, zoom,
You always try to scare me,
But you aren't scary,
You're just hairy.

The Strange Plant Pot
by Ciara Bradley

Last year, I went to my big sister's Nativity play in St. Vincent's School, Glasgow. After the play there was a raffle and lots of numbers were called out - 297, 998, 117 - and so it went on. Just when we thought we were not going to win anything, the lady called out, 'And finally, yellow ticket number 195.' We thought it was 194. '195 please,' the lady was saying.

Just then Mum said, 'That's us!' My little sister and I went up to get the prize. We didn't have a clue what it was. The lady gave us the prize. It was so funny. It was a plant pot with eyes, a nose, mouth, legs and arms. We went back to Mum. She said, 'What's this?' Then my mum and gran burst out laughing. We all went to get a drink.

Emer's teacher asked, 'Do you like your prize?' Then the teacher started laughing. We went home and showed the prize to Dad.

He said, 'I am not using that!'

The strange, funny plant pot is still sitting in its box in the garage!

Out of Sight
by Gary McGuinness

My big black insect is fat and scary,
As it creeps along its legs look hairy,
It's very quiet as it climbs up the wall,
Slowly moving through the hall,
It moves towards the bedroom,
Out of sight,
I won't see it again tonight.

My 8th Birthday
by Caitlin McCormack

On the 30th of December 2003 I had a sleepover with 3 of my friends named Shannon, Amy and Ciara. This sleepover was to celebrate my 8th birthday, which wasn't until the next day. I couldn't have my party on the 31st of December as this is Hogmanay.

My friends came to my house at 6 o'clock on that night. It was the first time they had been to my house and I was really excited. I had put on my party clothes and put make up on and glitter on my hair. My mum and I had blown up lots of balloons and put up a Happy Birthday banner in the living room.

The first to arrive was Ciara. Her mum dropped her off and she had brought her sleeping bag and pyjamas with her. The next to arrive was Shannon and then last to arrive was Amy. They had got me a present and I was really excited and dying to open them but my mum said that I had to wait until the next day because it wasn't my birthday until then. Once my friends had all turned up and put their sleeping bags away in my room, my mum told us all to put on our coats as we were going to the Ten Pin Bowling. I just couldn't wait. All of my friends said they had been to the bowling before and enjoyed it. When we got there my dad tried to get a strike for us. He got one for us and one for Amy. In the end Amy won. After that we went home. When we got home we got our pyjamas on. We went down and got some food. We had prawn crackers, chocolate and pizza. We went upstairs and carried on. After that, we got our sleeping bags and got into them, said our prayers, and we watched Daddy Day Care until 10.00 PM then turned the TV off and talked until 3.00 AM. We all fell asleep and woke up at 10.00 AM.

Don't You Fall
Rachael Maxwell

Little insect on the wall,
Go away or you might fall,
Down the wall you will fall,
In my hair for a little crawl,
Don't creep on me or I may weep,
Then I will not sleep,
And if I don't sleep,
I can't count sheep,
So please little insect don't you fall.

Rachael Maxwell

My Favourite Memory
by Laura Seggie

My favourite memory is when I made my First Holy Communion last year. I stepped out of my car and walked up the steps to St. Augustine's. I walked down the aisle and over to get my photo taken. I walked over to the sacristy and went in. We had to wait on chairs until the rest had come. A few minutes later my best friend Alexandra came. We had to wait a few more minutes, then everyone was there. Then it happened. I went out, down the aisle and went and made my First Communion. I read out a reading. I was a bit nervous at first, but then I was fine. Later on my Mum, Dad and my little sister were there. We went in our car to the place we had my party in. I felt happy and glad I got to go to Communion at church.

Beth
by James Chisholm

One day I was coming home from school and I saw my Mum in a taxi. I realised she had come from the hospital. Then I went back home to tell Dad. But when I got home my Mum was already there. So I went in to see the new baby. My Mum told me it was called Beth and she was a girl. A couple of minutes later Martin came home and Mum told him her name. It was the greatest day of my life, I had a wee sister. Then my big sisters came home and they also got told her name. Everyone in the family was happy and for a treat we went out for dinner, and also had a good night's sleep, especially Beth.

Archie Smith, Boy Wonder
by Ryan Morgan

One frosty September night, Archie Smith clambered into bed. He was absolutely exhausted. He was just home from his best friend Adam's birthday party and was rather relieved to get into his big soft bed. It was quite a cold night and Archie couldn't get to sleep. Suddenly over at the window hollow lights were glooming in the dark. Archie didn't dare to move. He sat bolt upright like a statue wondering what it was. In a split second flat there was a flash of light that blinded Archie. A shadowy figure stood right in front of him. It was an evil magician! He flicked his wand three times and a time warp vortex opened right in front of his very eyes. Archie bolted for the door petrified of what might happen. But he was too late. The vortex sucked him and the magician up. He cried for help but the magician had put a spell on his parents. After a lot of spinning Archie was transported to a horrible looking castle and was locked in the deep, dark dungeon. But Archie grabbed an axe, broke the lock, ran up the rotting staircase, destroyed the evil magician and jumped through the vortex.

First Time Home
by Evan Traquair

My little brother covered in a shawl,
He looks like a tiny doll,
With his big blue eyes.
He loves to play with my school ties
All day long.
And to make him happy we sing a little song.

The Witch's Spell Part One
by Alexandra Donald

In a dark spooky corner stood a hideous cupboard, its cracked shelves full of slimy bottles and jars. Grizelda the witch ran a scabby finger across the page of a spooky spells book. She gave a spooky laugh and stirred the dusty cauldron. As she chanted horrible words the scabby cat sat by the fire watching her. Grizelda hated children so she put up a candy store so the children would come and poison themselves. She put in poison sweets and eyeball juice, the juice tasted like apples. Then she dressed up as an old gran to fool the little children.

The Witch's Spell Part Two
by Philip Arcari

The witch next took an empty bottle and scooped up some of the potion and gave it to her cat and the cat turned into a duplicate of her. As more cats came, more duplicates came until there was no more potion. There were enough witches to rule the world. Each of them had a two metre broomstick and a ten centimetre wand. They went out zapping people. They all turned into witches and wizards. They put all of the houses together and made a five hundred million foot castle. The castle was so big it blew up and all of the duplicate witches dissolved into ashes. The witch's potion failed as usual. And she was so angry, she blew up as well.

Wishes
by Melissa Liner

As Archie fell asleep three fairies came in the window and in a small voice one of the fairies said, 'He is the one.' He started to wake up but he fell back asleep. The fairies went over to him and lifted him by the arms and legs. They took him to fairy land. He thought it was a dream, but it wasn't. The fairies granted him three wishes. His first one was to take him back home. The second one was that he was never here. But he kept the other one for a special moment. The fairies took him back home and put him back in his bed and he fell back asleep. The fairies decided to give him another three wishes and when he woke up in the morning he found the other three wishes on his shelf. He gave them to his Mum, but his Mum said they weren't real. But she made a wish and it came true and that is how the story ends.

Cute Little Babies
by Larissa Woods

Cute little babies
Have cute little ways,
Cute little babies
Have a cute little gaze,
My cute little baby has days
When he's not so cute.
That's when he cries,
And he cries,
And you can't press mute.

My Mum
by Evan Traquair

My Mum is no
Ordinary mum,
The best mum in the world,
Her eyes are golden brown,
Everytime I do something
Right, she gives me a surprise.

Sister
by Vicki Cunningham

Sporty
Intelligent
Smart
Tall
Excellent at singing
Responsible

Father
by Ryan Morgan

Fantastic,
Always does nice things with me,
The best man in the Universe,
He's brilliant,
Excellent in every way,
Really, really, really, really, really, really great.

The Locked Attic
by Amy Wallace

Once upon a time there was a lady called Nicole. She had two children. Her eldest daughter was Nicole and her youngest daughter was Amy. One day she bought a house in Maple Street. It was a very old house. It had been empty for fifty years. That night they sat on the couch.

'Mum, can I go out on my bike?' the wee Nicole said.

'No honey, we have lost the key for the lock for the attic,' said the big Nicole.

'OK!' said wee Nicole.

Then George came in and said, 'Where are my children?'

The two children ran and jumped on him like monkeys. George ran upstairs and burst the attic door open. 'There you go,' he said. But the light wasn't on, so he pressed the switch at the side. He heard a funny noise. That minute the house vibrated and went up then up. **3 ... 2 ...1**

Blast off!

The Deadly Book
by Calum Watt

One day I had to go to my aunt's house for two weeks and because I did not have friends there, my friends Michael and Iain and Steven came too. So we had to go on a boat to a little city. When we got to the city my aunt was waiting for us. She took us to her house. When we got there we went for a walk to a big library. So we went into the library. We saw this strange man. We went over to talk to him. We were talking for a while and then he showed us all of the books. Then he said to us to look after the books. So he went to get his lunch. A boy came into the library. He took the book that the man said not to give away.

Steven said, 'Do not take that.'

But the boy took the book away and we followed him. But when we got to the door he did not let us warn him. The next day we chapped on the door and we asked his mum and dad if he was OK. But they said he had not woken up yet. The next day an ambulance was there.

We went to the boy's mum and dad and we said, 'What is going on here?'

'Our boy is dead.'

We all said, 'It was the book!'

When I Am Bored
by Collette McKeown

Nearly everyday I am bored. I am bored when I have nothing to do. But when I am bored I go and watch TV. If there is nothing on I go and play with my dog or my toys. I go up to my room and read or listen to a CD. But if that is boring I just watch TV even though I don't like anything on it. Or I go out to play. But if everything is boring I just wait till the next day. And the next day I go to school and that is not boring!!! But I hate when it is hometime because when I am in the house it is boring. Every day is a school day, but Saturdays and Sundays are not. They are the boring days of the week. School days are the best.

Bart Simpson
by Dale McCaul

He is a yellow summer morning,
And he lives in the skate park.
He is a lovely summer day,
And he is a spiky chair.
He wears an orange top and blur shorts,
His TV programme is Itchy and Scratchy,
And he is a bowl of jelly.

The House On Maple Street
by Eve Robertson

One dark and cold night on Maple Street when no one was outside, there was a strange noise then something fell from the sky. When it dropped it made so much noise it woke everyone up. They all ran out of their houses to the police station. As soon as the police heard they thought everyone was making it up. But they ran out and saw an old bashed house. They ran in to investigate. There was no one there so they went back to the police station. And then the people heard something else. There were police cars and helicopters everywhere. There were ropes to lift the house up. Then they sat it down. A young couple came to buy it, so they did.

I'll Never Understand Humans
by Iain Kane

I was in the supermarket buying messages when I heard shouting. So I went to see what the fuss was about and I couldn't believe what I saw. A witch was complaining to the manager because the supermarket had nothing she wanted. She wanted to know who would want to buy the silly things on their shelves and what type of witches came there to shop.

The manager said, 'Sorry Miss, you're the first witch who's shopped in here. No one's asked for bats, slugs or bugs before.'

The witch replied, 'That's the last time I ever come to the store. I'll never understand humans!'

The One Ring
by Jack Mulholland

It is gold,
It is a winter's night,
Fires of Mount Doom,
And a rainy day.
It is a burning table,
Steel armour,
And the Return of the King.

Opposites
by Lewis Kane

The sky is blue, grass is green,
I've plenty more opposites if you're keen.
Dark and light, day and night,
The dark may fright,
But the light's all right.
Big and small, wish I was tall,
Fat and slim? Glad I'm thin.

Me
by Megan Cannon

Hello, I'm Megan. Let me explain to you what I look like. I have red hair and blue eyes. My family is pretty big. My wee brother has short blond hair and big blue puppy dog eyes. Well, I remember something else. Snowball, our little kitten. She is white and has bright green eyes. Oh no! My wee brother Owen wants me to play Nintendo. When I play Nintendo I win. It is so boring. After that I just lie in my bed and read till my mum says, 'Meg, time to go to your gran's.' But then my gran goes to Asda and that's when it gets so boring. I scream my head off till my granddad says, 'I'll take you to McDonald's when your gran comes back.' Till then I ride on my bike.

I need my mum to sign my homework. My aunt walks in and talks for ages and ages. So I go into my room and read and read and read till I am out of books.

The GO Button
by Michael Vallely

One day me, Calum, Dale, Ciaran, Adam, Piero, Lewis, Blair, Jordan and Brandon were living in a house. Adam noticed a button and it said **GO**. He told Calum and Calum said, 'Don't touch it.' We all thought it might be a button to make the house fly or we could do magic. Later, we were having a pillow fight and Blair hit Jordan and Jordan fell downstairs and his back hit the **GO** button. We all stopped.

'What's happening?' said Jordan.

'Stay calm,' said Dale.

'We'll be all right,' said Lewis.

The house started to shake!

We looked out of the windows. We couldn't see

anything except tiny houses and people. We thought it was cool but wee Ciaran said, 'You better watch out we don't hit anything.'

Brandon noticed that we *were* going to hit something. It was hot.

I said, 'Watch out! It is the sun.'

We tried to stop but we couldn't, so we all jumped out of the house. Then we were all safe and that was it.

My Mum
by Nicole Loran

My Mum is gold,
My Mum is winter,
My Mum is a busy shopping centre.
My Mum is a sunbed on a rainy day.
My Mum is a summer's day dress,
My Mum is Charmed,
My Mum is a cup of tea.

My Dad
by Nicole Meechan

My Dad is yellow because he is a cool summer's day,
And he is a toy factory,
And he is a pair of jeans,
And his TV programme is the football,
And his place is the chair,
His food is a curry,
And he is a box of red roses.

Barry McLees

How I React
by Hugh O'Hear

Some people react to insults by panicking and nearly screaming.
Others react by hitting someone.
I walk away.

Some people react to compliments by blushing.
Others react by shaking and getting embarrassed.
I laugh.

Some people react to bad news by panicking.
Others react by just worrying.
I shiver.

Some people react to a joke by shouting.
Others react by saying, 'Very funny.'
I laugh.

Some people react to sudden noise by screaming.
Others react by twitching.
I shake.

The Coatbridge Vikings
by Nicole Mulholland

Fifty years from now there will be a family, a Viking family. The dad is called Ben the Red Beard. He is obviously called that because he has a red beard. He also has brown eyes, red hair and he is thirty years old. The mum is called Beverley. She has brown eyes, brown hair and she is twenty eight years old. Their little girl is called Amy. She has red hair (like her dad), brown eyes and she is eight years old. The story started when Amy started to cry. 'I want to see my granny. I haven't seen her in ages.' (This is because Ben's mum lives in Norway and Ben lives in Coatbridge.)

'Ben, when are we going to visit your mum?' Beverley shouted upstairs to Ben.

'That's what I wanted to talk about dear. I am going to make this house into a spaceship,' Ben said as he raised his voice.

'Stupid Daddy,' Amy said. 'You can't make a spaceship.'

'Yes I can,' shouted Ben. 'You wait and see.' So Ben stormed off. Beverley and Amy didn't see Ben after that. Then one day he came into the house and screamed, 'I did it!'

'Show us then Honey,' said Beverley calmly.

So Ben took Amy and Beverley into the garage. 'Ta da!' Ben said as he pressed a button.

'Three, two, one ... take off!' said the machine.

'Weeeeeee.' said Amy. 'This is fun.'

Then Ben pressed a red button. 'Oh no,' Ben said quietly.

'The spaceship is landing,' the machine said over and over again. Then **BANG!** the spaceship crashed and Ben, Beverley and Amy all said together, 'Where are we?' Then they all looked up and saw a sign saying *Welcome to Russia* and at that minute they realised they were stuck there forever.

Monkey Slippers
by Lauren McLeary

I saw a monkey in the shop,
She was looking for some slippers,
She saw some pink ones on the shelf,
Just the thing for her big sister.

Under the Rug
by Nicole Watt

At 19 Haddington Way there was a man called Mr Watt. Mr Watt was always in a rush because his cat, Smudge, never let him out the door. One day he arrived so late for work he only had two hours to work. He should have been working for five hours. He was so tired he nearly fell asleep. When it was time for him to go home he ended up getting a taxi because he was too sleepy to drive.

He unlocked the door and he put his dinner on. He said, 'I wonder where Smudge could be.' Then Mr Watt saw something under his rug and it was *moving*. It followed every step he took! Mr Watt ran upstairs and fell into bed.

The next thing he knew, his alarm clock went for work. Without thinking, he forgot all about the thing under the rug and all about where Smudge had got to. He even forgot about breakfast. He had to phone for another taxi because he had left his car at work the day before. But he dropped his phone ... there was that thing under the rug! Mr Watt screamed and ran upstairs and then he ran back down. The thing that was under the rug tried and tried to get out. Mr Watt got a knife and cut the rug ... and out ran Smudge!

Mr Linden's Library
by Peter Donaldson

Sarah was a non-believer. She didn't believe in mysterious happenings or myths. One Friday 13th of October Sarah was going to buy a book. She went to her uncle's library. Mr Linden was a strange man, but Sarah didn't mind. Her Uncle warned her: 'Don't leave this book open, whatever you do.'

'Yeah right Uncle,' said Sarah.

As Sarah was going to bed that night she thought she would have a read. About a quarter of the way through the book she started to get drowsy. After a couple of seconds she fell asleep and did exactly as he uncle told her not to ... she left the book open. Sarah was never heard from again.

'If only she hadn't left the book open,' said Mr Linden solemnly with tears running down his cheek. How did she disappear? We may never know ...

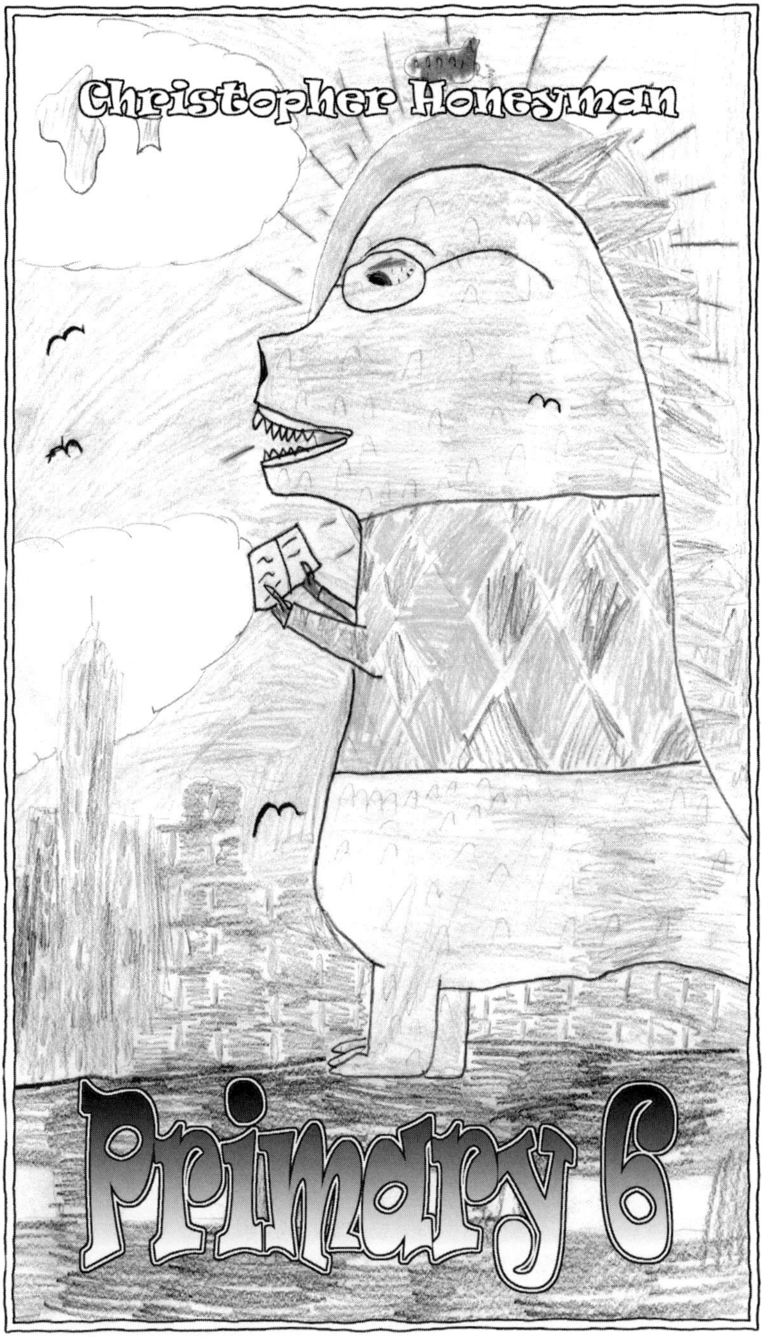
Christopher Honeyman
Primary 6

Autumn
by Lucy Kirkland
and Hollie Ferguson

Rustling leaves, blowing wind,
The leaves are red, brown, orange and green,
Evergreen I used to be,
But now I'm brown you see,
People pass me everyday,
Children climb on me and play,
Here I stand all day and night,
Hidden in the bushes out of sight,
It is quiet and calm all day long,
People pass, singing songs,
I wish it could be me walking along.

Hope
by Samantha Donnelly

Hope is pink,
It smells like a rose,
Hope tastes like a fresh strawberry,
It sounds like graceful music,
It feels like a relaxing bubble bath,
Hope lives in a mind of an Angel.

Hate
By Nathan Craig

Hate is dark brown,
It smells like cold-blooded flesh,
Hate tastes like blood from the human race,
It sounds like the scraping of the blackboard,
It feels like the grinding of your teeth,
Hate lives in the centre of the Earth.

One Dark Night in the Wrong House
by Lynsey O'Hear

It was a cold dark night on Friday the 13th. I was out wandering about the town. I was in and out of shops buying gifts just before the shops closed. It was nearly ten o'clock when I came out of a shop. There was a power cut so I headed back home. But I accidentally went the wrong way and entered someone else's house. I walked about thinking, 'This isn't my house.' Then I spotted a set of stairs so I ran up. There were lots of doors so I decided I would check them.

Then when I was walking towards a door, I noticed that there were lots of portraits. Their eyes looked quite real and when I looked back the eyes were looking at me! After a while I saw a door that was different. I went over and tried to open it. It was locked but beside it there was a set of keys. I picked up the keys and opened the door. When I walked in it was really dark. I turned on the lights thinking they would only last a couple of minutes because of the power cut. I turned round and saw people hanging. I was scared to death.

I screamed as loud as I could and ran but I was too late, there was someone standing in the doorway. I tried to get away but I couldn't. He locked me in. I tried to grab the keys but they were too far away. I tried to make something to grab the keys with and I succeeded. I opened the door and ran everywhere looking for a phone because I had to tell the police about *him* but the line was cut off. I ran to the police station and told them about the murderer and he got arrested.

Hope
by Sinead McMullen

Hope is yellow,
It smells like lemon,
Hope tastes like fresh fruit,
It sounds like calm music,
It feels like the gentle touch of God,
And it is like inside a daffodil.

Paint Box
by Jamie McAnulty

Red is a rose on a summer's day,
A heart on Valentine's Day,
Blood on a sword in a battlefield,
Traffic lights on a busy road.

Blue is mould on an old loaf of bread,
Cold feet on a winter's night,
Blueberries on a spring bush,
Fishing and swimming in the sea.

Green is the stem of a lovely flower,
Grass on a hot summer's day,
Leaves on a nice tree,
A bush with jaggy nettles.

Yellow is the flowers in a lovely spring garden,
The sun like a lolly in the sky,
A lemon nice and juicy, ready to eat,
A banana in a jungle on a tree.

Deadly Encounter
by Johnathan Maguire

It was on a dark night me and my mum were
driving home from a party. Then there was a loud
bang and the car skidded and stopped. My mum tried
to start it up again but it was no use. We got out of the
car and went to look for help. The wind was howling
and it was freezing cold. Then we stopped and there

was a house in a field with some lights on. We climbed over a small fence and started to walk up the field. When we reached the house it was old and spooky. I rang the doorbell and someone answered. It was a tall man with grey hair and a wrinkly face. My mum explained what had happened and he invited us in. Inside the house was old and dull with lots of dusty pictures. There was an old woman sitting next to a warm fire.

The man took us into a room at the back of the house and told us to wait. Then he came back and asked us if we wanted anything to eat but we said no. Then he went away again and suddenly the whole house went pitch black. I grabbed the back of my mum and said, 'What has happened?'

She said, 'There must have been a power cut.'

We walked out of the room but there was no sign of the man or woman.

My mum said, 'Let's get out of here.' We walked down the hall. There was a creak and we ran into a room. Suddenly a candle lit and the woman in the living room was lying in her chair with a knitting needle through her neck. Me and my mum screamed and then the man was standing with a knife in his hand.

My mum grabbed me and we started to run for the front door but it was locked. Then I saw a glass door. My mum saw a blanket and put it over us. We ran and jumped and we smashed right through the door. We flung the blanket off us and we started to run. The man was gaining on us. But we caught sight of the car. My mum got the keys out of her pocket and pressed the button to open the car. We got in and locked the doors. My mum tried to start up the car. The man began hitting the windows. She eventually got it started but didn't realise the man was in front of the car. She accidentally knocked him down. She kept on driving and when we got home we reported it to the police. Two weeks later they got back to us and said the man wasn't dead but he was arrested.

A Boy Called Bill
by Paul Kerr

There was a boy called Bill,
Who jumped off a windmill,
He broke his leg,
And found a peg,
And met a new friend called Phil.

Misery
by Ryan McGonigle

Misery is the colour of darkness,
Misery smells like oil,
Misery tastes quite muddy,
Misery sounds like children screaming in the dark,
Misery feels quite creepy,
Misery lives in a basement so they say.

Brogan's Paint Box
by Brogan McMullen

Green is a snake slithering along,
Grass so fresh in the morning dew,
Leaves flickering in the breeze,
Trees so tall and green.

Red is the colour of blood pumping through my body,
The heart on a Valentine's card,
So big and full of love,
Red is the colour of strawberries so juicy,
It is also the colour of roses so pretty
To make your garden look pretty.

Yellow is the colour of the sun,
Glistening in the summer,
Lemon sherbet, so sour and fizzy,
Yellow is the colour of the daffodil bright and fresh,
A spring chicken so fluffy and small.

White is the colour of cloud so soft and cuddly,
Snowflakes falling so soft on your skin,
An igloo as icy as your freezer,
White is soft as a feather.

War
by Kieran Elliott

War is red,
War smells like death,
War tastes like smouldering batter,
War sounds like a machine gun,
War feels like pain,
War lives in the heart of the Devil.

When I Was Young
by Christopher Honeyman

When I was two I was eating chocolate and it went all over my hands. I didn't know what to do so I thought for a moment and saw the glass doors. I ran over to them and wiped my hands on the glass. My mum sent me to my room.

I was about three when we went to Toys 'R' Us and I got a new tricycle. When we got home I ran upstairs, got my helmet on and went outside. I got on my bike and went along a little bit. Then I lost my balance and fell off. I was crying and nearly broke my ankle.

Another time when I was three I went to my gran's. I was running up and down the stairs. My mum said, 'Be careful.'

I said, 'I will.'

My mum went into the living room, then she heard

a **THUD!** and she came running out. I had hit my head off the radiator and passed out. That's all I can remember.

When I was eight I went to Lanzarote. My mum and dad said they had a surprise. When we got there I saw a submarine. My dad said, 'We're going on it.'

I screamed, 'Yes!'

When we got in I looked for fish but only saw an angel fish.

My First Day At School
by Brian Crossan

It was 1998. I was so nervous I got out of bed and went to the bathroom, washed my face and brushed my teeth and then I got my new uniform on. My mum did my tie. I had my breakfast and then went to the bus stop.

I got on the bus and sat down on a seat and the bus pulled away. I was so nervous. The bus stopped and I got off and walked to the gate. I went into my new class and a boy came up to me and asked me what my name was. I said my name was Brian. I asked the boy's name and he said John. He asked me if I wanted to play with his toys and I said yes. My teacher was called Mrs Lawtie and she was a good teacher. First she asked all our names.

We were allowed to play with the toys. It was playtime and John and I met a boy called Paul. We asked him if he wanted to play tig. It was good playing tig. When the bell rang we had to go in. Mrs Lawtie gave us a page of sums but when you finished it you could play with the toys. The bell rang and it was time to go home. When I got home I told my mum how much fun it was.

Things I Would Change
by Joseph Feeney

If I could change anything in the world I would stop vandalism because it destroys our towns. There should be more litter bins.

I wish smoking was banned because people die as smoke gets in their lungs and stops them breathing. I suggest they stop selling cigarettes, or stop making them. They should even make a law banning smoking.

The people in the Third World have little food or water. The water is dirty and they should dig more wells and send more food over in planes. As well as this they should have more food and money to buy good houses and have schools for their children and live a happy life.

They should stop wars, making weapons and then no one would die. The people who started the war should just make peace because it ruins other people's lives.

What I Am Really Like
by Scott Reilly

I can play football because I play for a football team and my coach taught me how to play football and he showed me so much that I became a good footballer. I like ice-skating because you get to play on the ice, it's really good fun and you get to go to the ice-skating disco. I also like swimming because you get to go down the chutes and go on the Rubber Ring Ride and into the deep water. I like riding my bike because you can go up the ramps and go bike runs.

I would like to be someone magic because you can do magic stuff and you can be a magician. I would like to be a professional footballer because you get lots of money, you get to play in football matches and you get to go to other countries. I would also like to be Tom Cruise because you get to go on boats, fly jets and you can be the Last Samurai. My favourite thing is reading books. The best story I have ever read is Treasure Planet because it tells you about a boy finding lots of treasure. My best television programme is wrestling because people dress up and fight, sometimes in cages, and win special belts. The best game I have ever played is my Playstation. You can play games on it and try to complete them. You can look at games in the shops as well.

What I like most about school is gym because you can play games and exercise.

Love
by Stephen Henderson

Love is the colour of deep red,
It tastes like fresh cream cake,
It smells like fresh cookies,
It sounds like birds whistling,
It feels like petals all over you,
It lives in a big castle.

War
by Jennifer Dornan

War is the colour of deep red,
It smells like rotten fish,
It tastes like burnt chips,
It sounds like the horn of a car,
It feels hard like iron,
It lives in the darkest corner of the Earth.

Peace
by Catherine Fraser

Peace is the colour of creamy white,
It smells like flowers blooming in spring,
It tastes like fairy cakes all laid out freshly,
It sounds like a heart playing sweetly,
It feels like hugging one thousand teddy bears,
It lives in the bottom of your heart.

Friendship
by Nichola Tuite

Friendship is the colour of bright yellow sunlight,
It smells like a sweet candy stick
Which you share with your friends,
It tastes like vanilla ice-cream with strawberry sauce,
It sounds like birds singing a sweet melody,
It feels like you're in heaven,
It lives in the heart of someone special, my best friend.

War
by Thomas McDonald

War is the colour of the darkest black,
It smells like a smoky fire,
It tastes all bitter and disgusting,
It sounds like a deafening bang,
It feels like a spiked cactus,
It lives in terrible hell.

How Octopuses Got Eight Legs
by Jamie Boyle

In the very beginning before the octopuses got their legs they had no legs. All of the other fishes were just the same as they are today. The octopuses couldn't catch fish because they had no legs.

Soon this changed because the octopuses were very hungry. The gods started to feel sorry for the octopuses. Zeus, the King of All Gods, chose to give the octopuses legs as a reward. The octopuses were full of joy.

And that is why even today octopuses have long orange tentacles and can easily catch fish.

How The Rhino Got Its Horn
by Catherine Fraser

In the beginning there were no animals on the earth except one silly rhino. All he ever did was roll about in the mud from the jungle. He was always getting dirty, but he never took a bath. He kept on saying to himself, 'When other rhinos come I will take a bath.' But no rhinos showed up. He just wished there were lots of other animals to keep him company. One sunny day he realised that whenever he walked past plants they would start to die down. He had a horn on his back that was starting to get sore. He had had problems with his horn for years. He finally decided to take a bath.

After a while he got home and pulled out a big bucket of water and went out in the dark, took his skin off and started scrubbing. He put his skin up on his washing line and waited for it to dry. When he put it back on and he noticed something odd and he felt just a bit different. He didn't bother about it but at breakfast time he saw his horn in an odd place. On his nose! He quickly reacted and tried to pull his skin off but it was stuck and it wouldn't come off! He was quite scared and wondered what had happened.

It was a disaster! He tried his best to ignore it but it was impossible. He eventually decided not to bother about it. He made furniture for himself and placed it in his house, he made animals out of wood and they kept him company. He grew fond of his horn and decided to keep it after all. And that is why, even today, rhinos have horns on their noses and that is how the story ends.

Halloween Horror
by Eamon Bradley

On the 31st of October 1986 at 8:00AM, I left my house to go to school. In school I drew lots of vampires and skeletons. As soon as I got home I got dressed into the cowboy suit I was going to wear.

I was just about to leave with my big bag and cowboy suit when my mum and dad stopped me. They looked strange and their eyes were whirly. They were hypnotised! I was wondering who had done that when a hand grabbed my back and knocked me out.

When I woke up I felt dizzy and when my eyes came back to me I saw a bat floating above me. I screamed and tried to run but I was trapped in a raft. I felt a pain sear through my stomach and I began to stretch. I roared with pain. I felt like I had been ripped through the middle of my body. And then I did hear a rip! But it wasn't from my body, it was from the bat that had been floating above me before.

I was shaking in my boots when I saw a vampire appear. The raft let go of me and I jumped up with fear.

The vampire spoke. 'Hello Eamon.'

I shivered and said, 'Who are you?'

'I am DRACULA!!!' he said, 'and this is my house.'

I looked around to see giant spiders staring at me but I had no time. I ran, never looking back. When I was back in my house I punched and kicked my brothers, my mum and dad. They woke up and said they should have gone to school as well.

Ghost Story
by Thomas McDonald

One night my friend Peter and I were allowed out late. We were playing on the swings when Peter said, 'Do you want to play on the tree swing in the park forest?'

'Okay then,' I said. So we ran to the forest quickly but we didn't see the sun go down.

It was quite dark, we noticed an eerie rustling in the trees and it made a scary sound.

'It's getting dark,' I said. 'I think we should go home. So, do you know what way we came in, Peter?'

He said, '… er … mmmm!!! I don't know.'

So we were lost and the trees seamed to bend like they were trying to grab us. Also a terrible howling sound echoed though the darkness. Just then I saw something gliding through the air like a spooky owl. A strange figure swooped towards us while shouting, 'INTRUDERS DIE!' Then I saw *It* had eyes of fiery red and teeth as sharp as pins.

'RUN!' I shouted. We both ran as fast as we could. Just then a fireball appeared in *Its* hands and *It* threw it, narrowly missing me. We kept running and *It* kept shooting fireballs. Finally we got out of the forest and on to the so unpopulated street, and the…whatever it was sort of just dissolved into thin air. And as for when we got home ... you do not want to know.

How The Turtle Got Its Shell
by Ryan McGoogan

In the very beginning of the world there was one little creature. But when the first storm broke free, the turtle had nothing to protect itself with. All it had was four legs and a small head. It was so scared in the storm that it was trying to find a place to hide until it was over. It couldn't find anywhere at all, so it kept on going round in circles. The little turtle thought for a moment, 'Why did God not give me somewhere to hide?'

After a couple of weeks another storm broke free and on that day he found a place to hide because he fell into a puddle of tar. He was so sticky he nearly stuck to the ground. But he didn't. He bumped into a tree and the tree cracked. A branch fell and stuck to his back and he called it a shell, and when the storms came he could hide inside it.

And that is why even today the turtle has its shell to hide in and that is how the story ends.

The Windmonster
by Caroline Harty

Four hundred years ago in the year 1603 lived a man called Hazan. Hazan was being chased by another man called Syad, the King of Agroban. King Syad had beheaded 246 people and made 2000 people slaves. Everyone was terrified of him. Hazan and his warriors were on their way out to sea, but King Syad shot cannon balls at their ship and the ship was falling all over the place.

So Hazan and his warriors had to swim ashore and ended up on an island called Forganza. The sun was beating down on them and they were so tired they wanted to go to sleep. Hazan came up with a great idea. It was that they could build a tree house for them to sleep in. It was night by the time they had finished. It was very spacious on the inside and large on the outside. Hazan was upset to leave his country but glad to get away from Syad and his army.

The next morning Hazan heard a thud so he and his warriors went into the village and it was an enormous dragon that was about 200 feet tall and had huge webbed feet, eyes like saucers, and as scaly as a fish, teeth as sharp as razors, claw hands and spikes down his spine. Grundy they called him. Grundy was jumping on houses and looking for people to eat. Hazan tried to get everyone to a safe place. He saw a cave so he told everyone to get in.

Thump thud thump thud thump thud. Grundy saw someone get into the cave and followed them. Grundy finally got to the cave and got so angry it started a small whirlwind and then it turned into a huge hurricane and it was going all over the island wrecking everything. Luckily everyone was safe in the cave. A few minutes later they assumed it had gone and went out. But the hurricane started back up and they just got in the cave in time because a big tidal wave swept over the whole island. When everything had gone away for certain, Hazan and the warriors went out of the cave while the people of the island stayed inside.

They found the dragon eating trees. They surrounded him and captured him with their nets and got out their long, shiny, sharp swords and killed it.

But when they went back, the people in the cave had gone. They had disappeared and nobody ever found out what happened.

The Task
by Adam Flynn

It happened ten thousand years ago. A poor man called Claudius was walking in the woods one day. It was quiet and he could hear the birds chirping. He was just about to turn back when suddenly there was a black puff of smoke. When it had cleared away Claudius saw a man standing in front of him.

'Who are you?' Claudius said.

'I am the god Zeus,' he shouted.

'What do you want?'

'I hear you are a very poor man.' Zeus said, 'and I have noticed for the past year you have helped lots of people. So I would like to help you.'

'But how?' said Claudius.

'You must go to Mount Doom and bring me the diamond of fire.'

'And what if I *do* bring you the diamond? How will that help me?'

'I will give you all the money in the world.'

Claudius thought for a moment and then he said, 'Okay!'

Claudius got a map and set off. The map showed Mount Doom. It was very far away and Claudius knew he would be walking for a very long time. It started to get darker and much colder. He had been walking for hours and then he finally reached his destination, Mount Doom. It was very tall and the only way to get up was to climb. Claudius remembered what Zeus had said to him before he went on his journey. He had said the diamond was at the very top of the mountain. About an hour passed and finally Claudius got to the top. He was walking around and something caught his eye.

It was a glowing light in a cave. Claudius thought that would be the diamond. He walked into the darkness of the cave but he stopped as he heard something growling. Suddenly he saw four red eyes staring at him. He ran out of the cave into the light. A giant creature jumped out of the cave after him. It was a two headed snake. It pounced at Claudius, but he dodged the creature. He brought out his sword and fought this creature. He ran as the creature tried to bite him. Claudius knew it would be very hard to beat the creature. He had an idea. He ran behind a wall and lit a match. He threw it in the creature's eyes. With it not being able to see it would be easier. Claudius climbed up a little bit further until he reached the exact top.

The creature could not see him, so Claudius quickly grabbed the diamond, climbed down the mountain, ran through the woods and finally caught up with Zeus.

'You found it!' Zeus said. 'Now you shall be rewarded.' Suddenly bags and bags of money surrounded him.

'I must leave you now.' And with a puff of black smoke he was gone. From that day forward Claudius lived happily ever after.

The Dangerous Animal
by Callum Lyons

'Come on,' said Stephen.

'No way,' said Jack.

'Who knows what might happen?' said Mark.

'Oh don't be silly,' said Stephen.

'But something might happen, like we could get caught. Or something could escape,' said Mark.

'Nonsense!' replied Stephen. 'Besides, I know an easy way in.'

Mark and Jack agreed.

So that night they went to the zoo.

'So how do we get in?' said Jack.

'Just follow me,' replied Stephen. So they followed him round the corner, where he moved a branch, and they went through a hole in the wall. They started to explore. After a quite a long time they heard a growling noise.

'What was that?' said Mark.

'I don't know,' said Jack.

'Oh don't be such a wimp,' replied Stephen. They went on, turned a corner and saw that one of the cage doors was open. Then they looked around and saw huge footsteps in the hay. They were freaked out. Next they heard a roar. Stephen looked round the corner with his heart pounding and saw a dark shadow. He pulled his head back, then looked again and it was gone. The boys started to run and turned around the corner. Suddenly they froze in fear as there in front of them was a huge tiger, with an arched back, snarling teeth and sharp eyes.

'*Ahhhhhhhhhhhhhhh!*' they all screamed.

Scrambling to their feet, they ran in the opposite direction. The tiger darted after them. The terrified boys fled until they thought they'd lost it. But then it pounced right at them. But Stephen had cleverly led them back to the tiger's cage. The tiger leapt through the air. At the last moment Stephen slipped to the right and, unable to stop, the tiger went headlong into its cage. The boys quickly closed the door and locked it.

And then they went straight home.

Pitch Black Saturday Night
by Ross McLuskie

It was a pitch black Saturday night, even for seven in the evening, and I was on the phone to James and David, who were twins, about the haunted mansion.

'See you at eight,' said James excitedly.

'Ok,' I replied.

At eight o'clock I met them at the Boregarde Mansion.

'So, you two ready?' I asked.

'Yes,' said James.

'No,' whimpered David.

'Wimp,' muttered James.

'Are you calling me a wimp?' David exclaimed.

James couldn't be bothered answering him, so he punched him on the nose and knocked him out. We went into the garden and it got colder the closer we got to the mansion.

'This feels weird,' said James.

'Shadows!' I shouted.

We got into the house and I heard eerie footsteps upstairs. We ran up the creaky staircase and there was a huge black figure standing cackling.

'I've found it after all this time. The world's most valuable diamond!'

'Hold it right there buster!' we all shouted, grabbing the gem off him and fleeing. We saw shadows in the dark and lots of people jumped out at us. James had been caught! I ran as fast as my legs could carry me, round the corner to the police station and handed in the diamond. I told the police that James had been abducted. So they drove round the corner and raided the house. A few moments later they brought James out alive and well. What a relief!

Autumn Says
by Fiona Dewar

Trees are bare,
Leaves are spare,
At night in my bed,
Autumn just says, 'I'm here.'
The snow is almost falling,
And the leaves are crawling.

Freak Street
by Lucy Kirkland

One day last year in a house in London at Number Forty, Freak Street, two girls called Emma and Emily were at the park. They lived with their mum and dad. Emma was tall and thin with blue eyes and brown hair. Emily was small and thin with brown eyes and black hair. Emma, like her dad, enjoyed scaring people. Emily was like her mum, who hated being scared.

It was the night before Hallowe'en and they were out playing.

'Girls, it's time to come in now. It's getting late,' their mum shouted across the road.

'Ok,' replied Emily. 'Come on, Emma, we'd better go.'

'Ok,' replied Emma, who was quite annoyed.

As they walked over, Emma thought of an idea. Emily went into her room and Emma went to hers. As night fell, and Emily lay there quietly sleeping, suddenly there was a creak, creak, creak from the stairs. Emily woke frantically. 'Oh no, what was that? Who was that?' she thought to herself. As time went on she tried to get back to sleep. She heard more noises heading for her room. Emily was so sacred she didn't dare open her eyes. Her door opened. Things moved about. She couldn't think who it was and she nearly jumped out of her skin. She turned round to maybe have a look and found there was nobody there.

'Is anyone there?' she whispered. No answer. But the weird thing was Emma slept through. As morning came Emily got up, but there was a trap and the only person in the house who made traps was Emma. 'Mum!' Emily shouted.

'What is it?' said her mum.

As mum came in goo, water, mud and a lot of other stuff fell on top of her. 'Emma!' shouted her mum.

'Yeah Mum?' answered Emma calmly.

'Why did you do this?' demanded her mum, trying to calm herself down.

'Ooops,' she said timidly. 'I didn't mean to.'

'What do you mean?' she said.

'Ok, I'm sorry. I just wanted to scare Emily,' she said. 'And it was very funny. I mean, she didn't know it was me.'

'It's okay, but please don't do it again,' said Emily.

'Okay,' she said.

'Well Emma, you can get this cleaned up while I get washed,' said her mum.

'I will,' said Emma.

Shadows in the Dark
by Emma Boyle

One dark, stormy night as I was trying to get to sleep, all I could hear was the rain beating the ground and a howling gale of a wind. I am Laura Main. I have dark, bushy brown hair and baby blue eyes. I am tall and thin even though I am only eight.

It was so difficult to sleep. Suddenly I heard a creaking noise that was very creepy. I saw a human shaped shadow. Scary, I thought. A whip of thunder made me jump out of my skin. I crawled out of bed reluctantly to see what the shadow was and keeping quiet I crept out of the room. I spun to my left and saw a huge shape towering over me. But I shook my head and noticed it was our cabinet in which we kept the china. I spun to the right and saw a long thin shadow. A broom! I felt extremely silly. There's nothing to be frightened of. After that I was sleeping like a baby and not scared anymore.

'The end,' said the chairman.

'Aw, can we not hear more stories?' moaned the camp children.

'No!' said the chairman. 'Go to bed and don't be scared by the shadows,' he laughed.

Nightmare Shadows
by Kerri Innes

One dark night a howling gale was blowing. Rain fell like spears and thunder cracked like a whip above the clouds. Emily was in her bed and her mum and dad were in bed too. There were fast asleep but Emily was wide awake. She was watching a video and saw something move. She looked out her window but there was nothing there.

She went to the toilet and when she came back there were shadows, dark shadows, all over her bedroom. She was scared, very scared, petrified actually. She tried to ignore it and watch her film, but she couldn't. They started moving, but she just kept on watching her film. Then she put her covers over her head.

All of a sudden, she woke up, scared to death. She said to herself, 'It was only a dream.' The next morning she told her mum and dad and dad said, 'I went into your room to turn off your video and you were fast asleep.' Emily felt so stupid.

Bonfire Shadows
by Daniel McHugh

It was a dark night and it was as cold as a polar bear's underpants. My dad, Jonathan and I went down to the park to build a bonfire. We met my friends who were playing football. I told them about the fire and they wanted to help. We went to collect wood, paper and anything we could find for the fire. After we gathered the things we needed my dad went to light the fire. The fire was burning fiercely. When we were standing around the fire, we saw an extra shadow. We turned on the torch and saw someone. But all of a sudden, the torch flickered and went out. We tried get it to light again but failed.

We all wanted to go home but we were all too scared. About five minutes later, we all ran to my house and had some food. Then all my friends were taken home by my dad.

Great Things
by Ruth Locke

It was a beautiful African night. Leigh and I were staring out at the sunset. We had only arrived a couple of hours ago and already we were entranced.

'What a brilliant way to spend the summer,' Leigh remarked.

'Mmm,' I mumbled back. In Scotland the sky was always a grey-blue but this was super!

Leigh stretched and looked at me. 'I'm really tried, Becky. I'm going back to camp.' She yawned a last time and strolled away.

'Not without me!' I flung my legs back over the wall and we walked into the dark forest together.

As soon as we walked to a tall, thick tree, Leigh stopped. 'What was that?'

As soon as she said it, I saw it. A tall, young man, with jet black hair, was riding on the back of a giant mammoth. I gasped. Weren't they supposed to be extinct?

As the pounding of large feet grew louder, Leigh grabbed hold of me. 'Let's go back to camp!' she begged. Sweat was dripping down her pale cheeks.

'No, I want to see this,' I protested. I knew this was a one-off experience. Leigh's nails dug into my shoulder. The mammoth's feet sounding like a whole stampede. I was petrified. If it came any closer it would crush us. Leigh was in shock as her body shook. The steely eyes of the mammoth met mine. It had seen us!

The ground shook. Leigh screamed. The sound of her feet told me she had run away. I was on my own now to face my fear. My heart pounded so fast, I felt as though it was going to burst out of my rib cage. As it came closer I was horrified. The beast was huge. '*Aaaarrrrggggghhhh!!!!*' I boomed as I shot off as fast as I could. I needed to get to camp and fast! But as soon as I ran, the mammoth sounds were gone.

I got back to the camp at one in the morning, Leigh was there but sound asleep. I didn't stop for her. I desperately needed to consult the tribe leader.

'Excuse me sir, but I was in the jungle and I saw this young man and a mammoth. What is the meaning?' I questioned.

'Young Becky, you should not worry, it's a legend that if you see it, great things will become of you,' he answered. He was very wise and I knew it. 'Now get your rest or you will never see the flamingoes in the morning. So I went.

I'll never forget, great things will become of me.

The Dangerous Animal
by David White

One dark night in winter, Charles was watching television. It was cold, dark and everything was white with frost. Charles is ten years old, he is very brave and confident and all his classmates think he is very funny. He has blond hair, blue eyes and wears glasses. Suddenly there was a loud thud that made the whole house shake.

Charles looked out of the window and he saw something, something huge, coming up the road. Without a thought, he ran out of the house and dashed into a nearby forest. He only looked back once to see his house turn to rubble. Charles kept running and tripped over a rock.

It was very, very dark and Charles could just see the moon up through the trees. Just then, Charles saw someone sleeping against the tree. He approached him slowly. He was just next to the person when a huge clawed hand burst through the trees, grabbed the person and pulled the man out of the forest. Charles could hear a scream, the munching sound of teeth and then … silence.

'Oh my gosh,' Charles shouted.

He stood there petrified. Just then the trees opened again and a huge scaly face with sharp yellow teeth gazed into his eyes. Charles was terrified. Then the creature turned around and walked down the road. Soon it was out of sight. The street was a mess, but it was rebuilt in a few months and Charles would always remember that day. He would never, ever forget it.

The Wet Toddler
by Susanne Flynn

Drip, drip, drip, drop, cuckoo, cuckoo.

It was eight o'clock and my bath was ready. I didn't want to go in, you see. As I was only four, I ran into my bedroom and hid under the most obvious place … the bedcovers!

'Susanne, your bath's ready, I'm coming to get you!'

I laughed into my mattress. My mum had spotted me. Uh oh! She threw back the covers and scooped me up. I still had my pink dress on plus my socks.

My mum sat me down in the bath. I stared at my dress. Then … pop! It inflated! I burst out laughing. My mum said I laugh so much, my face turned red. I was in the bath for about an hour playing with my Barbie dolls and singing at the top of my voice. I must have had a sore throat after that.

When it was time for me to get out, I was dancing about with little water drops following me. My mum crept up behind me with a towel and grabbed me in her arms and got me ready for bed.

And that's the end of the wet toddler.

David White

Hernan Crespo
by Brendan Rafferty

Hernan Crespo is blue,
He is a hot summer's morning,
He is Stamford Bridge,
He is the crashing thunder,
He is a goal machine,
He is the Premiership,
He is a big bowl of corn flakes.

My Big Brother
by Bernadette Donnelly

My big brother is groovy green,
He is a hot summer's day on a wild football pitch,
He is scorching,
He is a fresh Celtic top waiting to be worn,
He is a comfy sun lounger,
He is Sportscene,
He is a bowl of fresh ice cream.

Treasure of the Caribbean
by Michelle Mulholland

In was 1988 when I went scuba diving for the first time. I was very interested in seas and oceans and wanted to explore the Caribbean. I went on a really big speedboat called *Horizon* along with my diving partner Alice and soon we were able to jump in.

At first it was cold and it felt really weird breathing out of a tube. We swam down together until we were at an acceptable level. It was beautiful. There were hundreds of fish which I studied and the place felt magical. There was the striped parrot fish, the cardinal soldier and a huge shoal of fish weaving in and out and side to side. It was a sight to see. There were so many fish bustling along, going about their business. The butterfly fish, angel fish, clown fish and lion fish created a fantastic atmosphere. We began to swim further down and something caught my eye as it sparkled beautifully.

Leaving Alice behind, I swam further down to see what it was. I didn't notice how deep I was going until my bones started to hurt. The water pressure was strong, but I still wanted to see what this was. When I reached it I felt as if my bones were cracking. I put my hands out to find it was gold coins. I looked up and saw Alice coming down to meet me and with the little power I had left, I tried to swim up. But I was weak and things began to slow down.

I woke up in hospital. The nurse said had I stayed a further minute my life would have been over. However, I still have the gold coins which have been examined by experts and may have belonged to a famous pirate.

The Sun
by
Ashleigh Wallace
~

The Sun is big and hot.
It gives us light and heat.
It lives up high in the sky
With all the clouds.
The sun is a member of the
Solar system with the
Earth and lots of
Other
Planets.

Poems
by Emma Sharkey

Poems rhyme,
Poems make songs,
Poems make you
laugh even if you're
sad.

Everyone
likes
a poem
once
in a
while.

Exploring the Deep
by Leigh Cairns

I shall begin my story in the summer of 1990. I was a wealthy woman and my friend Ashleigh and I decided to hire a boat to go on a journey of a lifetime.

Exploring the deep in the Pacific Ocean. With deap blue seas and skies while the sun beats down. Ashleigh and I set off for our journey on the 22nd of May. We had stocked the boat with provisions but the crew made light work of our supplies. The Captain, Ashleigh, myself and our eight crew set off out the harbour while our family and friends all waved in nervous anticipation of our dangerous journey ahead.

We were soon in the Pacific Ocean when we saw a family of dolphins playing with each other.

Our anchors were lowered. The time had come for Ashleigh and I to put our equipment on. The crew helped with our breathing apparatus and we were slowly lowered. That's when it got really exciting and we dropped into the wide ocean.

When we were in the ocean we saw colourful schools of fish, in many shapes and sizes .There were lots of animals which blended in with the seaweed and shells. As we were coming back there was a dolphin; it was so shiny. I could hardly believe I was finally exploring the deep.

Kingswood Lake District
by Danielle Mullen

It was August the 31st, one day after my birthday, and I was going on holiday. It was something like an adventure. The bus was leaving from the school the atmosphere with the families was amazing. There was half of Primary Seven and a few others from school. It was two hours travelling and it was really fun reading magazines, eating sweets and talking.

When reached England we had trouble finding the Kingswood Lake District. The sign was so small though you would think that it would have a big sign.

When we arrived my stomach was rumbling with nerves. I was really excited and glad to be in a dormitory with my friends. We were there .... everybody clapped. We saw some Problem Solving that looked challenging to do and we also saw Caving, Quads and other things. We got off the bus with bated breath, waiting to see what we were going to do. They gave us two letters where we would line up every morning after breakfast. Our house was called Ullswater house and our animal name was RABBIT. After coco at night my nerves were up to my eye balls and I wasn't missing my mum. Kerri was so annoying with her daft talking. She and Amanda are mad together. Kerri had brought her torch for us. When the lights went out it was so cool. Everybody felt up for a party but for a starter there was no music. So I was the one who told everybody to be quiet or else we were all going to get sent home.

Next morning we had Site Central which was interesting. We where doing Interactive Stories after that juice break. Then back to activities: Nightline when you got blindfolded and held on to a rope and then crawled through tyres and even Mrs Fraser poured water over us. Then lunch and you got to play for half an hour and then back to activities. The next activities I can't really remember but were fantastic.

It was the same routine over and over but different activities. My favourite was Laser Tag where you had to shoot. My team won. My second favourite was Teen Challenge where you had to work as a team. The other fantastic and cool one was Caving. I didn't really like it because of enclosed spaces but it was great fun in the end. It was like exploring. I was really sad leaving Kingswood and I would really love to go again.

Tiger Woods
by Darren Campbell

He is red,
He is a fiery hot summer's day,
He is St. Andrew's Golf Course,
He is a thundery blast,
He is a red top,
He is a comfy sofa,
He is Sky Sports 2,
He is a bowl of ice cream.

Colours
by Lynsay Wallace

Red is the colour of a big juicy apple,
Blue is the colour of the sparkling sky,
Brown is the colour of dead petals falling,
Yellow is the colour of the sun shining down on us,
Green is the colour of the Christmas tree standing tall,
Orange is the colour of the ginger street cat,
Purple is the colour of the dark, scary sky at night,
Black is the colour of a wicked witch's hat,
Pink is the colour of my heart pumping every second
of the day.

The Magic Pencil
by Joseph Weatherall

One rainy day in 1957, when it was as cold as a polar
bear's underpants, Philip Mannering and his sister
Dina were going on an adventure holiday to the Isle of
Gloom. Philip was small with red hair, lots of freckles
and had a parrot called Jay Jay. Dina was tall with lots
of freckles and red hair. So when they packed they set
off for their holiday. Four hours later they arrived at
the harbour, but the ferry was delayed for one hour.
They eventually arrived at half past five in the
afternoon. The captain gave them a free map of the
island and they found out that there were diamond
mines on it.

Philip and Dina built a house made of willow
branches tied at the top to make a roof. They filled the

walls with heather and bracken, which wasn't easy. The next day they put their stores in a nearby cave which they had found earlier that day. Later they went onto the diamond mines and went down to have a look. While they were down Philip found a pencil, so he picked it up and waved it. Just then a box of chocolates appeared in Dina's hand, a packet of parrot seeds in Jay Jay's mouth and a pair of football boots on Philip's feet, with his trainers now in his hands. He waved it again and a bouquet of roses appeared in Dina's hand, a dozen mice at Jay Jay's feet and a cluster of diamonds in Philip's pocket. He didn't want to wave it again because they had too much to carry, so they went home.

The next day they woke up in Buckingham Palace with the crown jewels on their bodies. He was so worried he shook it again and they were back in their own beds. Then Philip heard a knock on the door. It was an elf. He had pointed ears, long blond hair, a bow on his back and arrows in his pocket. He had come to get his pencil back and he asked politely. He said he would give them a million gold coins for it, so they gave it to him and shared their gold equally.

Daydreams
by Nicole Luchini

Mr Martin thinks I am reading,
But I am swimming at the bottom of the sea,
I am walking on the moon,
I am flying in the sky,
I am invisible and slapping people in the face.

Mr Martin thinks I am listening,
But I am walking through hot lava,
I am sailing a ship,
I am wrestling a duck,
I am riding on a fox's back.

Daydreams
by Rebecca Henderson

Mr McGoo thinks I'm reading,
But I'm flying a powerful aircraft,
I'm diving in hot lava,
Or chasing shooting stars,
I'm wrestling frying pandas.

Mr McGoo thinks I'm listening - but no,
I'm standing on top of the Eiffel Tower,
I'm leaning on the Tower on Pisa,
Or making the Mona Lisa smile,
I'm soaring through space,
Or starting a fight with Rocky.

Pele
by Mark Hughes

He is yellow,
He is a fiery hot sun,
He is the roaring Maracana Stadium,
He is a gale force wind blowing down defenders,
He is the coolest pair of trainers ever,
He is an extremely powerful electric guitar,
He is the whole Soccer AM Review,
He is a spicy chilli.

Balde
by Declan Cowell

He is black,
He is a fiery hot summer,
He is Celtic Park,
He is a stormy wind,
He is Black Magic,
He is a brick wall,
He is the Scottish News,
He is a welcome bag of chips.

There Was
A Man Called Fred
by Frankie Martin

There was a man called Fred,
He's dead.

Anne Robinson
by Lee Kearney

She is black,
She is a boring grey sky,
She is the Weakest Link,
She is a rainy day,
She is a boring black dress,
She is a dark chair,
She is on the TV,
She is a big lump of porridge.

A Fantastic Time
by Jennifer Stone

It was the night before the September weekend and I was really excited and had also gone a bit hyper because the next morning I was leaving to go to Blackpool for a day with most of the people from dancing class. I couldn't wait but I had to go to bed early because we all had to meet up at seven o'clock in the morning in the Time Capsule car park.

The next morning I was dancing about wildly because today was the day. I was over the moon; I just couldn't wait any longer. I got dressed, had my breakfast and my mum and I set off for the bus. I got on the bus and most people were already there. About five minutes later the engine started revving up. I waved my mum goodbye as we set off for a long and tiring journey. It took us about three and a half hours to get there.

When we got there I was overjoyed. We went up to the reception, got our wristbands and set off for the rides. I went on the Grand National and that was great because our carriage won. Next I went on the Crazy Mouse and that went really fast and turned very sharp corners. Later I went on lots more rides and went to McDonald's to get something to eat. When we went back I decided to go on the Pepsi-Max, which was twenty-three feet above the ground and went eighty-five miles an hour. We were waiting in the queue for quite a long time but when it was our turn I was really scared. I didn't know this, but the ride took your picture and I looked really scary in the photo. When it was time to go home I didn't want to go. When I got home I fell asleep as soon as my head hit the pillow and I thought it was the most fantastic time ever.

Helen Webster

A Camping Nightmare
by Emma McAleer

Last year in America, around March, Lisa and Tom Perkins decided to go camping in Blackstone Forest about ten miles away. Former campers say they have heard, and some saw, strange and mysterious animals but it didn't bother Lisa and Tom. A few days later Tom and Lisa's dad drove them to Blackstone Forest and found them a spot in a small clearing and then left them to set up.

There were trees all around them, about twenty-five feet high, they felt so small and insignificant standing next to them. First they pitched their tent and lay down the ground sheet. Later on they went to find some wood for the fire in the forest. It was vast and quite eerie.

That night they were sitting next to the fire getting a heat when rain started to thunder down on them. They ran into the tent for shelter. A storm was stirring as the night grew on. Eventually the wind and rain was so fierce that it blew the tent away. Lisa and Tom ran into the forest and found shelter under a large drooping tree, but they were petrified. They started to hear growling noises in the distance. They came closer and closer. As they were looking out to the dark dense forest, a wolf walked past taking no notice of them. It turned its head and started to walk towards them and

Tom and Lisa walked back but could go no further. They took a run for it with the wolf chasing after them. When they eventually got out of the forest the wolf was nowhere to be seen. As soon as they could they got home. But that was the last camping trip EVER.

My Feelings
by Brian Boyle

I am happy when I am at a party,
I am horrible when I wake up too early,
I am puzzled when I try to do a crossword,
I am excited when it is Christmas,
I am bored when the TV is broken,
I am calm when I am on my own,
I am kind when I feel happy,
I am sad when I get hurt,
I am afraid when I watch horror movies,
I am curious when something is missing.

Colours
by Anthony Burke

Gold is the colour of the gates of Heaven,
Orange is the colour of the boiling hot lava in a volcano,
Black is the colour of the dark witch's lair,
Silver is the colour of the mythical unicorn,
Red is the colour of rich, dark blood,
Brown is the colour of the tar from a cigarette,
Green is the colour of the emerald so rare.

Making the World Better
by Scott Cutmore

I believe there are lots of ways to make the world better. First I'll talk about the people of the world. Racism is one of the most disgusting things, it is not civilised behaviour. World peace is another big thing. Some members of Parliament are not right in the head. Going to war is not on. You should gather all the world leaders around one table and talk about world peace.

The second thing is the environment. People don't want to walk around their cities and breathe in smoke and air pollution and they don't want to see litter. The seas and the rivers are all polluted with rubbish which leads to the death of lots of creatures. Factories should be cleaned up and inspected each month.

The third and final thing I am going to talk about is justice. Fair shares of food, warmth, water and money are needed. People can't live without these things and have a right to them. Parliament has money coming out of its ears, so forget the debt of the Third World countries. Regarding law and order, I feel that the death penalty should be brought back for those who deserve it. These are the ways I could make the world better.

The Last Word
by Anthony Boon

You've read our stories,
You've read our poems,
And witnessed our imaginations,
Of which, you really must confess,
Are full of revelations.

So now we must bid farewell,
And take our leave of you,
But readers please don't despair,
We've gone to write a book or two.

~

*This book would not have been possible without the
generous support of the following companies:*

EST.D 1846

Dewar's

*John Dewar & Sons
would like to congratulate
Saint Augustine's
and the Jam Neck team
on a wonderful initiative.*

*We hope the book
is a great success.*

MEDIA AFFAIRS CONSULTANTS
" With the creative touch"

Press

PR

Travel Features

Business Features

Photography

6 Orchy Crescent,   4 Forsyth Street,
Airdrie,   Airdrie,
ML6 9QN   ML6 9DL
Tel/Fax: 01236 602417   Tel/Fax: 01236 758215

Mobile: 0777 8989150
Email: acespindoc@aol.com

R. Murphy Construction
Block - Paving Specialist

"Myrtlebank"
97 Clark Street,
Airdrie ML6 6DU

Tel: 01236 756382
Mobile: 07836 636721
Fax: 01236 756383

**Unit 42, Evans Business Centre,
Belgrave Street, Bellshill ML4 3PN**

**T:01698 743068 F:01698 743080
www.bstcourier.co.uk**